THE UNDISTURBED SOLDIER

A Chancel Play

Ed Irsch

THE UNDISTURBED SOLDIER

2105/ISBN 0-89536-602-9

NOTES

Characters

MOTHER: a cook in the high priest's house
RACHEL: her daughter
MARCUS: the soldier
DEMITRIUS: a soldier

Scene I

Thursday   (after the arrest)

Scene II

Friday   (before the crucifixion)

Scene III

Sunday   (after the resurrection)

Setting

All scenes take place in an area between the kitchen ("door" is stage right) and the outside ("door" is stage left.) A bench or two may be added.

Presentation Choice

Each scene may be performed during a worship service on the designated day, or the three scenes may be performed as one play.

Playing Time

Thirty to forty-five minutes

SCENE I: Thursday

(MOTHER, RACHEL, MARCUS, DEMITRIUS)

MOTHER: *(Offstage in kitchen.)* How many times do I have to tell you —

MARCUS: *(Backs into area from kitchen, inserting "But . . . but.")*

MOTHER: *(Enters, continuing without a break.)* — stay out of my kitchen on Thursdays.

MARCUS: One cake. That's all I had.

MOTHER: Special cakes from the High Priest's kitchen are not for the likes of soldiers like you. *(Exits.)*

MARCUS: *(Still facing kitchen.)* But it was only one.

RACHEL: *(Enters through "outside door" muttering.)* Now who is upsetting mother.

MARCUS: *(Continuing while edging cautiously toward kitchen door to see if MOTHER is coming back.)* And it was delicious.

MOTHER: Don't try to flatter your way out of this one, Marcus . . . *(MARCUS has suddenly backed up because he realizes — from the nearness of MOTHER'S voice that she is about to re-enter; RACHEL, who is attracted to MARCUS, reacts to hearing his name.)*

MOTHER: *(Continues without taking a breath, entering.)* . . . you should have known I made just enough this batch and you spoiled the count.

MARCUS: *(Realizes she means it.)* I'm sorry. I really thought you made extra *(Now beginning to exaggerate.)* like you usually do for the starving soldiers.

MOTHER: *(With mock sternness.)* Just remember the one day a week the kitchen is off limits. *(Exits into kitchen.)*

MARCUS: *(Pause; not loudly, but trying to get in the last word.)* I have a short memory. *(Satisfied he has the last word, turns.)* Oh! Rachel. I didn't know you were here. How long have you been standing there?

MOTHER: *(Enters.)* You can remember other things. Rachel, try to talk some sense into this soldier. *(Immediately turns and begins to exit.)*

RACHEL: I'll try, mother. *(MOTHER exits.)*

MARCUS: *(After an awkward pause.)* I guess you've given up.

RACHEL: I . . . well . . . I don't understand what you mean.

MARCUS: You were supposed to try to talk some sense into me. I guess you've given up.

RACHEL: I wouldn't know where to begin.

MARCUS: That's an open ended statement. Is there too much or too little wrong with me?

RACHEL: I mean, I wouldn't know how to begin.

MARCUS: Perhaps I should help you.

RACHEL: No! I mean, how could you admit what is wrong with you and not correct it?

MARCUS: That's easy. From all appearances, I irritate your mother because I like her cooking. But if I'd hate her cooking, I'd irritate her more. Why should I change from liking her cooking?

RACHEL: How can anyone talk sense into someone who thinks like that? Who has a convenient reason for anything.

MARCUS: I must have learned it from your people.

RACHEL: What do you mean: from your people!

MARCUS: Many things have happened tonight. Things that a Roman would never do to escape responsibility for his actions. But I wouldn't want to bother your pretty little head with . . . I mean, I wouldn't bother you with them.

RACHEL: That's just more of your convenient reasoning. If you really can't prove a point, all you say is, "I don't want to bother you with details," or "You wouldn't understand, anyway." Is that what Roman honor means?

MARCUS: Do you really want to know what your people have done?

RACHEL: Yes.

MARCUS: You probably won't believe it if I am the only one telling you, even though I am a Roman soldier. I heard it again tonight that you need two Jewish witnesses to agree before that testimony is considered truth in your law. So for your sake, I may as well bring in Demitrius who was with me tonight. Then there will be two witnesses. *(Goes to "outside door," calls.)* Demitrius! *(Pause so that he comes to door.)* Demitrius, come on in here.

DEMITRIUS: *(As he enters.)* Did you get the cakes?

MARCUS: That's not why I asked you to come in.

DEMITRIUS: You said she would be a push-over.

MARCUS: Listen to me. There are no cakes for us tonight.

DEMITRIUS: The old charm didn't work, right?

MARCUS: OK. OK! Maybe tomorrow. But now I have a different problem.

DEMITRIUS: You usually have a problem if the charm didn't work.

MARCUS: Will you be serious for one minute.

DEMITRIUS: Have I cracked a smile since I came in? No. So I must have been serious.

MARCUS: What kind of convenient reasoning is th--. Oh, never mind. All I want from you is confirmation that the things I am going to tell Rachel are true.

DEMITRIUS: Seeing that you are the only female in the room, you must be Rachel. Hi. Marcus seldom makes proper introductions. I'm Demitrius. A Roman soldier's word is supposed to be believed — but I wouldn't trust Marcus's word either . . . He told me he could get some cakes.

RACHEL: He did get one.

DEMITRIUS: Did you get one?

MARCUS: *(Reluctantly.)* Yes.

DEMITRIUS: Is there anything left of it?

MARCUS: *(Offhanded.)* No.

DEMITRIUS: Well, Rachel. Shows he's selfish but maybe truthful.

MARCUS: I know what I am trying to say to Rachel is true.

DEMITRIUS: And you just want me to agree with you.

MARCUS: Only if it is true.

DEMITRIUS: Without getting any cakes?

MARCUS: I didn't know a Roman soldier could be bribed.

DEMITRIUS: *(After a short pause.)* That's one for you.

MARCUS: Perhaps now we can talk, seriously, about things that happened tonight?

DEMITRIUS: OK. But why relive a bad dream?

RACHEL: What do you mean?

DEMITIRUS: When one person is to be arrested, two — maybe three — Roman soldiers are selected as the arresting party. Tonight, this so-called close follower of Jesus came with a whole crowd of temple guards sent by the chief priests and wanted practically the whole army assigned to him to arrest one person. Supposed to be a threat to Rome.

MARCUS: See. Your people used convenient reasoning to ask for a whole army to arrest one person.

DEMITRIUS: We were told that Jesus of Nazareth is the one to arrest. Someone asked if he is the one who had passed through parts of Jerusalem earlier this week, bringing out the crowds, and was hailed as the blessed Son of David. Another added he might be the one who chased the merchants out of the temple and then came back each day and talked.

RACHEL: That was a day to remember. The crowds — joyous — in broad daylight —

MARCUS: But kept in order by good crowd control of the Roman army.

RACHEL: Always the Roman army.

DEMITRIUS: "That is the rabble rouser," this so-called close follower of Jesus said. He wanted to bring out another crowd to watch him hail Jesus as master and give the kiss of friendship to the one who is to be arrested. He said he was doing it as a favor to the high priest so there would be no mistake.

MARCUS: Your people don't take responsibility for your actions: he blamed his actions on the desires of the high priest.

RACHEL: Does the action of one person reflect on the whole nation?

DEMITRIUS: We followed this so-called friend to a garden. Someone came to us and asked us who we were looking for. He was told Jesus of Nazareth, and he said, "I am he." No one could move forward; some seemed to be pushed back and down to the ground.

RACHEL: (To DEMITRIUS, *but pointedly for* MARCUS'S *benefit.*) This happened to the Roman army?

DEMITRIUS: Then came the kiss of false friendship and the arrest. We brought him first to Annas and right now he is being questioned out there by Caiaphas.

RACHEL: When I was out there before, I heard that one of the disciples of Jesus cut off someone's ear, but Jesus healed it.

DEMITRIUS: If anyone drew a sword, it didn't take him long to decide not to fight anymore. They all ran away as we arrested Jesus. I caught a glimpse of one of them as he was running and it seems as if he is now outside by the fire. He sounds like a Galilean. Others picked up on it too and accused him of being a follower of Jesus. You might say some even taunted him. I heard him deny it — twice.

RACHEL: (*Directly to* MARCUS.) You mean a Roman soldier would taunt someone — even if he is not arrested?

MARCUS: Only to help that person understand what honor is all about. But a Roman would never threaten or taunt a friend or use a friendship for his own purpose.

DEMITRIUS: Then, Marcus, think of some of the things you said while I was talking. You used what I said for your purpose instead of allowing it to be received without prejudice.

MARCUS: You're right. I am sorry, Demitrius. Rachel, I apologize. You are right. The actions of one person should not be counted against anyone else.

DEMITRIUS: Come Marcus. It's time to go. We must be ready to relieve others when the cock crows. It will be difficult — without cakes.

MARCUS: Yes. We may not make it though our watch.

DEMITRIUS: Say. Wait a minute. What do you mean WE may not make it?

MARCUS: What else should I say?

DEMITRIUS: You had your cake! *(Exits.)*

MARCUS: *(At "door" asking for confirmation.)* See you again, Rachel?

RACHEL: *(Short pause.)* OK. Fine.

MARCUS: Good! *(Exits outside.)*

MOTHER: *(Enters from kitchen.)* Well, did you talk sense into him?

RACHEL: No. But Demitrius did.

MOTHER: Demitrius? That's a new one, isn't it?

RACHEL: *(Hesitantly.)* Yes.

MOTHER: *(Deciding not to pry.)* I've been hearing about terrible things that are going on at the house. Do you know who has been arrested?

RACHEL: Jesus of Nazareth.

MOTHER: How did you know?

RACHEL: Marcus and Demitrius were in the arresting party.

MOTHER: At least they were in here during the questioning. I heard some of it from the courtyard and about some of it from the soldiers. Our high priest allowing — almost encouraging — witness after witness to testify. Finally when two witnesses said something about the temple, only Caiaphas could get a connection.

RACHEL: Sort of like convenient reasoning?

MOTHER: Something like that. But what was worse, the soldiers blindfolded Jesus and hit him; all the while saying to him, "if you are a prophet, tell us who hit you." This was allowed to go on in the presence of priests!

RACHEL: And you thought Jesus might be our promised Messiah.

MOTHER: But don't the Scriptures teach that the Messiah will be like a lamb when led to the slaughter? Jesus of Nazareth did not defend himself, and when asked if he is the son of God, he said, "Yes."

RACHEL: Then he is claiming to be the Messiah? The one promised to the world even before Abraham began our nation?

MOTHER: Yes. And he has been condemned to death. According to law as I know it, when the sentence of death is involved, there must be another trial the next day. But in twenty-four hours, the Sabbath will have begun. I assume the second trial will be delayed until at least Saturday night. If Jesus is the Messiah, it will be as Caiaphas said, "One person to die for all the people."

RACHEL: But how can the actions of one man be accounted to all people? I just made Marcus acknowledge that he should not look at the actions of one person and say that all of those same people are like that.

MOTHER: I didn't say we'd all be like him. But that he would act for us. It is as I have been taught by my father, a rabbi who believed that the prophets and Scriptures teach of a Messiah as a substitute sacrifice for all sins.

RACHEL: Even though your father (MOTHER *gives a look of displeasure.*) . . . I mean my grandfather was a rabbi, his belief seems to be another case of convenient reasoning.

MOTHER: You may call it that, but I feel there is a difference. The difference is faith. (*Begins to exit with* RACHEL *to kitchen.*)

RACHEL: Faith . . . or convenient reasoning. Which holds the truth? (*Both exit into kitchen.*)

SCENE II: FRIDAY

(MOTHER, RACHEL, MARCUS, DEMITRIUS)

MOTHER: (*Enters from kitchen with* RACHEL.*) I can't believe it. I can't believe what's happening this morning. I can't believe that Caiaphas did it.

RACHEL: Mother. If you said that once, you've said it a hundred times. I'm tired of hearing you say, "How could Caiaphas call the second trial of Jesus so soon."

MOTHER: It's not only that. He kept saying it was within the law because one trial was held Thursday night before the cock crowed and one trial this morning right after the cock crowed. At the first trial there was much testimony; at the second trial Jesus is asked one question before the council: Are you the son of God? An honest answer from Jesus and they call him a blasphemer, guilty of death. And now he's been taken before Pilate. They evidently need Pilate for something.

RACHEL: Are you still sure Jesus is the promised Messiah? You seem upset that he was condemned by the council to die. The Messiah is supposed to die, isn't he?

MOTHER: *(Gives RACHEL a hard look.)* It's just that I never expected his death would come because of lies. It doesn't change the hope in the prophecies.

RACHEL: *(Reacting.)* I know. I remember: Faith gives truth to hopes.

MOTHER: *(Really shocked.)* I can't believe it!

RACHEL: Oh, no. Not again!

MOTHER: No. It's not what you are thinking. I can't believe you remembered something I said. And do you know there is something you won't believe?

RACHEL: *(Guarded.)* What ...?

MOTHER: This time the extra cakes are ready for the end of the watch. There's enough for Marcus and Demitrius. I'm sure they will be here soon. Their watch is over. After we feed them, we are almost finished for the day.

RACHEL: Mother, how do you find out what is going on in the high priest's house?

MOTHER: I have ways. People seem to talk as they taste my cakes.

RACHEL: I thought they aren't supposed to talk with their mouth full.

MOTHER: They don't. That's when I ask the questions. Their answers come between bites.

RACHEL: But that still doesn't answer how you know what goes on inside the house.

MOTHER: Didn't you know that someone who knows the high priest is also a disciple of Jesus?

RACHEL: And he trusts you because you are really one of them.

MOTHER: I wish you wouldn't put it that way. I wish you could see Jesus as the promised Messiah.

RACHEL: I need more than faith that promises are being fulfilled. I need to see them fulfilled.

MARCUS: *(Enters from street with DEMITRIUS, brightly.)* Hi, everybody.

DEMITRIUS: *(Enters in an introspective mood.)* Good morning.

MOTHER: Marcus. Demitrius. You must be hungry after your watch. I made extra cakes — to make up for before. Would you like some?

MARCUS: You mean you're actually inviting us to have some?

MOTHER: Yes.

MARCUS: I can't believe what's happening this morning. Demitrius, are you coming?

DEMITRIUS: No. I'm not hungry.

MOTHER: Are you sure you don't want any? Not even one?

MARCUS: I wouldn't give him a second chance. *(Exiting toward kitchen.)* I'm ready. And hungry. I'm going. *(Exits.)*

MOTHER: Marcus. Wait for me. I don't trust you alone in my kitchen. *(Exits.)*

RACHEL: *(After an awkward pause.)* Why so . . . silent?

DEMITRIUS: I'm sorry. I can't believe what's happening this morning.

RACHEL: If I hear that phrase once more, I'll scream.

DEMITRIUS: What did I say?

RACHEL: Oh. Never mind. It's not your fault. It seems that ever since you left for your watch, mother has been saying, "I can't believe what's happening this morning." She rambles on about Caiaphas stretching Jewish laws. I don't understand it.

DEMITRIUS: I was talking about Roman justice not working and Roman honor being disgraced. I can't believe *(Notices RACHEL'S reaction.)* . . . Oh, oh. I'm sorry. What happened this morning doesn't make sense.

RACHEL: It sounds as if I'm going to hear about something, even if I don't ask about it.

DEMITRIUS: *(A bit flustered and hesitatingly.)* Not really. But I was hoping you might be interested . . . I mean . . . I was hoping you might want to hear about how I feel about things . . . that is . . . to hear about things that happened to me . . . that happened this last watch.

RACHEL: I'm a good listener. At times.

DEMITRIUS: I hope this is one of those times. I need to talk to someone. Any pride or confidence I've had in Roman justice is in a shambles right now. I was on duty when your Jesus . . .

RACHEL: *(Interrupting.)* He's not my Jesus.

DEMITRIUS: When this Jesus was taken from Caiaphas to Pilate. The chief priests practically ran us there. When they got Pilate to come out, they tried to make it seem they were doing Caesar himself a favor by bringing one of their own for trial. They said he was guilty of death because he claimed to be a king. We took Jesus inside to Pilate. Pilate asked a few questions and told the chief priests that the way Jesus made the claim, it was hardly worth a slap on the wrist, let alone the death penalty. As they tried to persuade Pilate to increase the penalty from a slap on the wrist, they mentioned that Jesus is a Galilean. With Herod visiting Jerusalem, Pilate claimed Herod had jurisdiction. Innocent is innocent; guilty is guilty. Pilate should have set Jesus free. Jesus came back from Herod with a purple robe. The guards laughed about how the whole company had mocked him. That was one instance of breach of Roman honor. Herod had returned Jesus without setting him free and without advice to condemn him. Not a trace of guilt, but Pilate said, "I will have Jesus whipped and then set free." Whipping an innocent man is a breach of Roman justice. Then Pilate received a message. The word in the ranks is that his wife urged him to have nothing to do with judging Jesus. The chief priests tried to push their case, but Pilate insisted on whipping only . . . then freedom for Jesus. He would not nail him to a cross. He thought he'd try the Passover release — that's what we call the custom he has of using the Jewish Passover celebration of freedom to remove the guilt of one hopeless prisoner and set him free. The choice that Pilate gave the Jews seemed foolproof to me. Perhaps Jesus would be set free after all. A Jesus was — but it was Jesus Barabbas — not Jesus the so-called Christ and king of the Jews. Then Pilate asked what he should do with Jesus. It didn't take long for the chant to start: "Nail him to the cross. Nail him to the cross." Pilate still insisted on whipping and freedom. But the chant gained momentum. "Nail him to the cross. Nail him to the cross." Roman justice is being forgotten; but it gets worse. I was there when Jesus was whipped and mocked. An innocent man being tortured. Roman honor disgraced. I made some weak excuse and didn't join in. Then the man — the innocent but beaten Galilean — was shown to the people as their king. Not even that could stop the chant. Again it came, stronger than ever: "Nail him to the cross." Pilate washed his hands and said he was innocent of the blood to be spilled. A Roman takes responsibility for his actions. He doesn't transfer guilt to anyone else. That is honor. Our watch was almost over and the additional duties in the next phase were extensive, so Pilate decided to change the guard. If Roman justice were not in a shambles, an innocent man would not be on his way to die on crucifixion hill. I don't understand what is happening this morning. *(A pause of at least six counts before he shows he realizes the words of his last sentence.)* Thanks for not screaming.

RACHEL: What do you mean?

DEMITRIUS: I said "that phrase" again.

RACHEL: Somehow it didn't bother me. *(Hesitatingly.)* But something else bothers me. Did . . . Did Marcus join in the beating and mocking of Jesus?

DEMITRIUS: I'd rather you ask him.

RACHEL: Roman honor at stake if you answer because you didn't join in?

DEMITRIUS: *(No reaction.)*

RACHEL: Enough said.

MARCUS: *(Entering with MOTHER.)* mmmmmm-**mm**! Those cakes were delicious.

DEMITRIUS: I apologize for not being hungry.

MOTHER: I think I've learned . . . I understand why.

MARCUS: Well, Demitrius, interested in finding out how they divided the seamless cloak?

DEMITRIUS: Not really.

MARCUS: Come on, Demitrius. Don't let it bother you. He was half dead when Pilate sentenced him. Probably did him a favor.

DEMITRIUS: That's only one way of looking at it. I'm going back to the barracks.

MARCUS: I'll see you later.

DEMITRIUS: Right. Let's go. *(At door, turns to MOTHER but speaks for RACHEL'S hearing.)* Is it all right if I get hungry another day?

RACHEL: *(Rather quickly.)* Please do. *(Catches herself.)*

MOTHER: Of course, Demitrius.

DEMITRIUS: I promise I'll get hungry very soon. *(Exits.)*

MARCUS: Thanks again for the cakes. *(Exits.)*

MOTHER: *(After he exits, sourly.)* Yes. Yes, Marcus. You're welcome. *(Having sensed a different awareness in RACHEL and DEMITRIUS.)* Anything you want to talk about?

RACHEL: Not yet. I mean, not really. I mean . . .

MOTHER: It sounds as if you're confused.

RACHEL: I am, mother. I am. And not only about my feelings. All these years I've been hearing about our promised Messiah from you, but not really listening. Is it true? Is Jesus the Messiah?

MOTHER: The evidence is in the meaning of the prophets. My father always reminded me of the words: He was led like a lamb to the slaughter and he didn't open his mouth.

RACHEL: That's what Demitrius described.

MOTHER: He was mixed in with criminals.

RACHEL: Jesus Barabbas and Jesus Christ.

MOTHER: More than that: he was led to Golgotha to be crucified with two thieves.

RACHEL: I didn't know that.

MOTHER: Jesus said that as Jonah was in the belly of the whale for three days, so will the Son of Man be in the belly of the earth.

RACHEL: Does it all fit for you?

MOTHER: Yes. Jesus is the Messiah. In three days he will rise to life. He raised Jairus's daughter; he raised the man from Nain; he raised a Roman centurion's slave; he raised Lazarus. He is Lord of life. Can you accept it?

RACHEL: Almost. Perhaps if I see him alive?

SCENE III: SUNDAY

(MOTHER, RACHEL, MARCUS)

MOTHER: *(Begins on stage with* RACHEL.*)* Don't you see, Rachel. There is a connection. "A gang of evil men is around me; like a pack of dogs they close in on me; they tear at my hands and feet. All my bones can be seen. My enemies look at me and stare. They gamble for my clothes and divide them among themselves." Another prophecy reads "But when I was in trouble, they were all glad and gathered around to make fun of me; strangers beat me and kept striking me." Isn't this an exciting time to be alive! The Messiah is Jesus. I know it. I believe it.

RACHEL: I could only begin to believe it if I would know he is alive, not before.

MOTHER: If you *hear* that he is alive, or see that he is alive?

RACHEL: It depends on who says what, mother.

MOTHER: We found out that even the captain of the guard said that he was really the son of God.

RACHEL: Right after an earthquake! Who wouldn't? But at this moment, we know Jesus is dead and has been dead for a couple of days. How can you be excited when there has been a death?

MOTHER: If you believed, you would be excited, too.

RACHEL: How can you expect me to believe when you said that all day yesterday the disciples — his closest friends — were meeting behind locked doors?

12

MOTHER: Locked doors seem to be the order of the day. Marcus and Demitrius are confined to quarters while part of the guard is assigned to Jesus' tomb. Which was also sealed.

RACHEL: You gather information from all over.

MOTHER: A few cakes, a good ear, and information is waiting to be plucked.

MARCUS: *(Enters through kitchen, holding something in a closed hand.)* Thanks for the cakes. I came through the kitchen and no one was around to ask. So, thank you.

MOTHER: Marcus. Those might have been set aside for a special purpose.

MARCUS: But this is a Sunday, not a Thursday. *(To RACHEL.)* Rachel. I have something for you. That is if mother — I mean, if your mother . . . will let me give it to you. *(Shows the gift of expensive jewelry in his hand.)*

RACHEL: Marcus. It's beautiful! But where did you . . . How could you afford such beautiful jewelry?

MARCUS: *(Not serious.)* I saved for it?

RACHEL: I know better than that.

MARCUS: Let's just say there are some very appreciative people in this world.

MOTHER: What do you mean?

MARCUS: Well, it didn't happen while I was on duty, but someone or some gang stole the body of Jesus.

MOTHER: How could that have happened, with Roman soldiers guarding the tomb?

MARCUS: I don't know. Probably one shift was over-tired, took a nap, and Jesus' disciples came and took the body. Now they claim he was raised to life.

MOTHER: You mean there is talk that Jesus did rise from death?

MARCUS: There's talk. But only from his followers . Their story is ridiculous. The body was stolen.

MOTHER: And you are suddenly wealthy enough to afford expensive gifts.

RACHEL: Mother. A Roman soldier would not accept a bribe. Demitrius said so.

MOTHER: If the jewelry is not the result of appreciation for knowing the correct story, then Demitrius must also be rich.

MARCUS: Not that . . . *(Catches himself before saying "fool.")* No. He's not.

MOTHER: How do you know?

RACHEL: Where is Demitrius? Is he still on duty?

MARCUS: No . . . He's . . . He's been transferred.

RACHEL: Transferred! Why?

MOTHER: *(Demanding.)* Where?

MARCUS: He's been transferred to Ephesus.

RACHEL: So far away! Why?

MARCUS: *(With the old "charm.")* Why not? Anyone who is able to keep the events of what happened this morning straight, stays in Jerusalem; anyone with any other story is transferred to the outposts. Immediately.

MOTHER: Like what other story?

MARCUS: The story of his followers, of course: about an earthquake, an empty tomb, and rising from death. How Demit . . . How anyone could believe that is beyond me.

MOTHER: Then we have the choice between the story supported by Roman honor . . .

MARCUS: *(Cutting in, adding.)* . . . and your priests.

MOTHER: *(Ignoring it.)* . . . or, in your words, the impossible claim of Jesus's followers.

MARCUS: How can there be a choice of truths?

RACHEL: Did you say Demitrius was transferred because he believes that Jesus rose from death?

MARCUS: I shouldn't answer for him when it involves beliefs. I can only say that he won't . . . I mean . . . does not support a reasonable explanation for the disappearance of Jesus's body. But what about the gift? Will you keep it?

RACHEL: You asked mother's permission before. She hasn't answered.

MOTHER: Whether to accept it or not must be your decision. I will not interfere.

RACHEL: Then you will understand if I ask you to leave us alone for a few moments?

MOTHER: Of course. *(Exits into kitchen.)* I'll be in the kitchen.

RACHEL: If I don't accept your gift, what will happen between us?

MARCUS: I shall think you don't believe me. That the gift is not honorable. That we can no longer be friends.

RACHEL: Must it be that severe? I thought you said that a Roman would never threaten a friendship once it is made.

MARCUS: There can be no friendship without accepting a friend's statements as true.

RACHEL: So it is with faith. There can be no faith without accepting that God's statements are true. But faith adds patience — as mother has told me many times. I'm sorry. *(Offering the jewelry.)* I cannot accept your gift.

MARCUS: *(Taking the offered jewelry.)* I'm sorry, too. *(Brighter.)* But it was fun while it lasted. Someone else will probably trust my statements and appreciate the jewelry. I may as well start looking right now.

RACHEL: Should I tell mother to continue making extra cakes for you?

MARCUS: I always came to see and talk to you. Talking with your mother was payment for the cakes. *(Going to outside door.)* I guess I should really be going now. Like I said, it was fun while it lasted and this is really good bye. *(Pauses at door.)*

RACHEL: Good bye, Marcus. Take care.

MARCUS: Thanks. You too. *(Cheerily.)* And, life goes on. *(Exits.)*

RACHEL: *(After a pause, goes to kitchen door.)* Mother, you can come back in here.

MOTHER: *(Entering.)* Rachel, what did you decide?

RACHEL: *(Factually, without regret.)* Marcus is gone and not coming back. Not even for your cakes.

MOTHER: I know you were attracted to him. How do you feel?

RACHEL: About Marcus?

MOTHER: Yes.

RACHEL: A little rejected. A little relieved. Mother, is there some way I could get away for while? To get my thoughts sorted out.

MOTHER: Any place in particular?

RACHEL: I was thinking, mother. Do you know anyone in Ephesus?

MOTHER: Why do you ask?

RACHEL: I've never been there. Maybe I'd like to see it.

MOTHER: Why the sudden interest in travel?

RACHEL: There's something I haven't told you. Last Friday, Demitrius told me Roman justice is in a shambles and Roman honor was disgraced. I want to tell him about God's justice and God's honor and God's taking over the responsibility for our sins.

MOTHER: *(Encouragingly, not disparagingly.)* And this will help you sort out your thoughts?

RACHEL: *(Becoming resigned.)* I guess it is a foolish idea. I know that I now believe Jesus is alive and is the promised Messiah. I think Demitrius knows Jesus rose from death but I wanted to find out what else he might believe. I guess it is too much to hope for.

MOTHER: What would you do if Demitrius doesn't believe?

RACHEL: I don't know. Come back home, probably. But I don't understand why I want to find out.

MOTHER: The answer may not be what you hope. Or the answer you hope for might take patience. Would you be ready for that?

RACHEL: I don't know. But I'd like to find out.

MOTHER: My cousin moved to Ephesus last year. I'm sure she would welcome you.

RACHEL: Would you allow me to go?

MOTHER: It looks as if God has already provided a way.

RACHEL: Then you won't mind?

MOTHER: Of course not.

RACHEL: It's wonderful. I don't understand what's happening this morning, but it's wonderful. *(Realizing something.)* Oh. But this means you will be alone. What will happen to you?

MOTHER: I'll stay here. There is no need for me to go. I feel God has a use for me right here where I've been and he will help me.

RACHEL: But the changes that have happened. I see everything in a new light. Demitrius has changed. Doesn't any of it rub off on you?

MOTHER: It has: a long time ago.

RACHEL: That's right. The truth you believed didn't change.

MOTHER: *(Cheerily.)* Truth goes on and life goes on. I've noticed you've mentioned the name of Demitrius quite often. Come! Let's have some cakes. *(Both exit to kitchen.)*

---

www.ingramcontent.com/pod-product-compliance
Lightning Source LLC
Chambersburg PA
CBHW081550040426
42448CB00015B/3275